Deep Snow Country

Deep Snow Country

BERN MULVEY

Oberlin College Press
Oberlin, Ohio

The FIELD Poetry Series, vol. 32
Oberlin College Press, 50 N. Professor Street, Oberlin, OH 44074
www.oberlin.edu/ocpress

Cover and book design: Steve Farkas
Cover art: Utagawa Kuniyoshi, "Nichiren Walking Through the Snow at
Tsukahara During His Exile on Sado Island." Allen Memorial Art Museum,
Oberlin, Ohio. Mary A. Ainsworth Bequest 1950.544. Reprinted by permission.

Library of Congress Cataloging-in-Publication Data

Mulvey, Bern, 1966-
 [Poems. Selections]
 Deep snow country / Bern Mulvey.
    pages cm. — (The FIELD Poetry series ; v. 32)
  ISBN 978-0-932440-46-4 (paperback : alk. paper) — ISBN 0-932440-46-0
(paperback : alk. paper)
  I. Title.
  PS3613.U456A6 2014
  811'.6—dc23
                              2013048337

To Yurina

Contents

1

わたしが一番きれいだったとき
街々はがらがら崩れていって

When I was at my most beautiful
city after city came crashing down

— Ibaragi Noriko

The Memory of Now

Memory is walking out a back door,
an evening garden, everything in its place
just the angles changing as one moves through,
each shadow, each shape new, set stones today
a stream frozen, forest lane, bridge across,
lantern a tower moss-capped, sentinel,
the *no* silent, suspended, azaleas
in season now, strawberry bouquets raised,
knotweed and dwarf pine, leaf blades a silver
shimmering. We'd sat right here, how it seems
just like it seemed, all strangely lit, candles
along the main road, sun but a crescent
pink above the mountain tips. The neighbors,
worried about us, had brought by crackers
and Kyushu tangerines, a care package
wrapped tight in the day's horrible headlines.
They stayed for our water and whiskey,
a last, hoarded box of Meiji's Almond
Chocolate. Four pieces each, we ate them
slow, our voices carrying like sirens
in that cold, that awful quiet. And then,
a shudder, branch still shaking as the bird
took flight, dark against a sky darkening.

How Not to Find a Body

Yamada, Japan, 2011

Focus on the small, a doll's right
foot, brass belt knobs, the brother glove.
Look for glitter, the reflected light
off pen tips, marble eyes, a card
case silver and empty. Listen,
the seagulls are out, the black crows
cawing, cacophony, circles
lower and lower around a
single point. Avoid them, avoid
the wide eyes of the old woman
calling and calling the one name,
the man sweeping a door-less stoop,
the boy soldiers with their full bags
in hands shaking. Forget the bus
over, how the lead volunteer
talked about protocol, tidal
patterns and probabilities,
on and on until the last hill
cleared, until an empty valley
opened beneath and all talk stopped.

Quake

Deep-boned, a grave sound
sudden as the first
thunder, ever late,

that says *begun*, though
it was always there,
the potential, air-

energy, this hard
liquid earth, the sea
a fist rising. Then

the chain rattle, the
rise up, each object
aware, buoyant now,

floor a carpet pulled,
again pulled, you the
constant, immobile,

the sky falling, one
consuming thought, *Save
something*, a human

answer, the question,
*What can possibly
survive this?* When the

silence comes we too
rise, a dust covers
us, the broken walls

weeping. Five minutes
it takes to leave, time
for two aftershocks,

a huge wave—we knew
nothing, power gone,
stairs a waterfall,

a slide, we walked hand
in hand, eyes blinking,
the glare as we walked

out.

Maho no Kotoba

*Literally 'Magic Words'—the name of the massive ad campaign
initiated by the Japanese government right after the earthquake "to help
maintain public order." Featuring animated animal characters singing
traditional Japanese greetings and honorific expressions, the commercial
repeated every seven minutes, interrupting important news broadcasts.*

Ohayo, the *what a great morning* eel
    says food and drink aren't coming
    but the river water
    should be safe.

Itadakimasu, the *I'll take that* rat
    says radiation levels
    are rising but not to
    panic please.

Ittekimasu, the *I'm out of here* skunk
    says the foreigners are all
    leaving aren't they a
    funny bunch?

Konnichi wa, the *good day* doggy
    says that things may be worse
    than reported but
    maybe not.

Gochisosama, the *wasn't that delicious* mouse
    says the spinach is still tasty
    just wash it baby
    wash it good.

Arigatou, the *thank you* bunny
    says kerosene for the stoves
    will be sent soon as
    the snows melt.

Tadaima, the *honey I'm home* sunfish
    says the neighbors have food
    to trade if we have
    clean water.

Sayonara, the *farewell* lion
    says Yamada is gone
    but don't worry we'll
    grow it back.

Oyasumi nasai, the *good night* rhino
    says that things will get
    better just say the
    magic word.

Gomi Station

In Japan, each street has its specified garbage disposal station, with a resident (usually elderly) assigned to make sure the correct items are thrown away on the correct day.

The day after yet still
out before dawn, five feet
in height maybe, back curved
like a question, iron-heeled
cane held ready to smite
crows, cats and worse, bringers
of wrong garbage. That day
the sun staggered up, stretched
light on a dark valley,
the quiet a fistful
of wool laid in a pan
filling with snow. That day
we were afraid to leave,
I watched from a window
her standing guard, the lone
wait, each breath a white veil
rising. It was a day
of smoke, fires unseen,
of aftershocks again
and again. When the truck
never came, when no one
ever came, she walked home;
red sky, the sound that cane
made on the ice-hard ground.

Tanka at the End of Everything

Miyako food tent,
my unsteady spatula,
the food edible
barely but the boy thanks
me thanks me again thanks me.

Two floors just girders,
steel, on the third candlelight,
laundry hung out. Clouds
moon-tipped and quick, a sea wind,
as people live in Yamada.

Unplanned, a father
alone at a parade end,
baby girl in one
hand, the other held high up
as his body spins and spins.

Train north from Tokyo,
a long tunnel, then before
the shades can come down,
elm, fir stands, sky electric
blue above Fukushima.

Tsunami Flooding
Expected To Here—lone sign
above Otsuchi,
valley below a mushroom
patch, intact roofs, steel stalks.

Highway 45,
sea wall there still taller than
what jumped it, silly
boat, the *OK* spray-painted
in red on its bared bottom.

Sansa Festival,
the Yamada old men dance
row upon row dance
until the crowd stands, their song,
echoing, shakes the earth back.

Fly-jin

Slang term, coined by the Japanese media, for the foreigners ("gaijin")
who fled Japan after the March disaster.

We were all confused, I by an ankle
that would not listen, that creaked at each step,
bending in the most surprising places,
they by the fact that I was there, big as
life, a pale abominable. Next I

was on my back, stick-leg strapped below
the x-ray bug-eye, a technician hunched
and sweaty beside me. Nervous fellow,
he wanted to chat up the monster, but what
to say? I watched his tongue dart in and out

of the tight mouth, touching the upper lip
as if the words could be found there. *When did
you get back?*, he asked finally, to which
I said, *From where?* Later, the doctor
was angry because I did not come sooner,

my ankle had gone to pieces, ground down,
shrapnel in the joint. Ten days I'd walked on
it, so much to do, everyone wanting,
needing to do something, Miyako gone,
Yamada gone, the very air poison,

my neighbor, 90 and carrying wood,
the kids searching for parents lost, calling
full names like resurrection charms, the men
at Fukushima, unnamed still, who stayed
behind, who disobeyed, they set the bar.

How when you ran
begins every conversation,
but I did not run.

Eclipse

A solar eclipse took place in many parts of Japan on May 20, 2012.

Everyone seems to know but me,
7 AM, the street is filled
with kids wearing tinted glasses,
faces skyward, paper and pens
ready. *What's up*, I ask one boy,
who sighs as boys do when adults
don't get it. *Nisshoku*—the sun's
eating, he tells me, which doesn't
help, then looks away, head shaking.
Around us, an agitation,
shadows slant, angel wings then thin
curves of light, the air tangible,
mist without fog, sky a cloudless,
deepening grey. A year later,
smiles of shade, parents in line,
their children sketching a hungry
star, how we assimilate loss,
how the blue pours back. Cruelly well,
the world works to be beautiful.

Afterward

       Like a mat lifted
shaken
             a dust rises
      over the city
                         rises
     until the valley
        fills
        until
               in that late afternoon sun
the fat-veined walls
the spring swans slow descent
                      river a mirror
the downed power lines sleeping
                    snakes
the single cloud a brush-stroked
               再
                        everything

     a flush
     a vermilion flame

2

死の国は鏡のなかにある

The Kingdom of Death lies within a mirror.

—Terayama Shuuji

Fall

Something fishy

                    wet

wake with the damn dog's
tongue up my nose
too early morning

                  but she's right

outside
kanpu

    the clawed wind
    which carries the first storms

blizzard incoming
deep snow country
drifts mongrel eye-high through March.
Time for a last walk
only us about
hoarfrost and quiet
air a pear just cut
maidenhair, maple and cherry
each tree its scent
its own sure theme of color
lemon, raspberry, peach and red wine
copsy roof
the ground padded
here with maroon leaves like five-point stars
there ocher and blunt-toed
a duck's webbed feet.
Now the dog hurries
that sixth sense they have of endings

      the road lamplit
      all horizons
      a smoke spreading the purest black.

For They Are Coming

mono no aware, *n*. 1. The beauty (pathos) that emanates from all
things
2. One's ability to understand this

The ceremony of insult
> *kutabare*
>> go to hell
> *shinjimae*
>> fuck off and die
>>> our son in fine form
> ten years short
> of eighteen
>> now on his toe
> tips
>>> red cheeks out
> a raging
> puffer fish

Year's end
> time
> to clean the graves
>> the newest the problem
> the grandfather dead
> the boy
>> unready
> for what's implied
>>> the ease of it
> present
>> to represent
>> a single stone
>> the hush of winter morning

Dentatsu   lightning in a field
                 now *communication*
                      the word
                      incandescent
                                there
          among the viburnums in the garden
                                again
          over the granite stepping stones he set
                                mononoaware
               meaning
               as energy
                      how everything now carries
               a charge of loss

Later
          the candles the boy must light
          sputter and hiss
          hitodama
                      the death fire
                 for they are coming
                 and the wind
                 brings their message
          the echo answers to the voice
          the heart distant
                 practices
                      practices
          its common work

21

The Author, Taken by His Boss to the Baths, Receives an Instructional Brochure

Less bath *how to*, more lost zen koan,
Good Matters, the reassuring cover,
Wash fist before entering, anthem
for lovers everywhere, the pictures
with their own lessons: balance a ripe
peach on your head, rinse and shine your ass
until sparks fly like stars, stand to piss
in the bath and see people grow horns,
the Japanese version different
from the first word, *youkoso*—welcome.

Oshita and I have said goodbye
to our wives, ladies to the red room,
boys blue, color of silence, lighter
than air, what rises as I enter,
rises to the ceiling and sits there,
balloon dog, mute tongue out. *Onsen s'ki?*—
Do you like baths? asks my naked boss,
silver-backed and not listening, one
foot already in the hot water.
I wash and wash but never come clean.

Booze Well

Our daughter gives us the look,
meaning *shut up*, meaning *don't
embarrass*. We're in conference,
her teacher's eyes are young,
placid, a thin brown as if
unused. My wife asks again,
the list, our daughter's name left
off, as with the welcome list,
the birthday list—a question
that begins and ends with *why*.

She is sorry, this teacher,
so much work to do, nothing
personal, you see, nothing
racist, the job impossible,
she tells us, then a sudden
smile, such a mix, such a rare
sound, is it common, this name,
where you are from—*Mo-ru-bi*,
she says, then before her hand
can cover it, a giggle

escapes, a hiccup. *Leaky
Day*, she says, meaning my name
in Japanese. *Sa-ka-i—
Booze Well*—I say her name back,
unwords all, queer pictographs
borrowed from China, *name*
itself *evening over mouth*,
fairy tale, a hand-me-down
that never quite fits, that we
pass on anyway, like hope.

Knuckleheads

My nine-year-old holds up
her latest, two red grooves,
parentheses, a boy's
tooth marks on the knuckles.
He asked for it—they all
do, hover and hair pull,
cooties and keep away—
they tell her to go home,
her answer is, *Make me.*
Tonight when her teacher
calls again, we'll talk boys,
though I know, being one
once long back, how we tease
those we like. My daughter
knows the drill, has out
the Band-Aids and ice cream,
hands a sticky mix, hair
long black onyx, her mom's
eyes and left hook, my...what?
Sweet tooth, big foreign nose,
Irish stubborn, causes
lost but loved still, certain
she belongs, that the right
words exist, the beauty
that could be conveyed if
we but chose to listen.

Dog

Not my idea, the beasts at home
of our own blood loud enough
and hungry, a growing problem
destined for the top shelves. Yet off
to the pound we go, and of course
we find something, a pumpkin puff
of poodle mutt marked *last day*,
up and up on its back stick-legs,
the grin we learn only later
is pain, a rib broken. While
we wait, on comes the quaintest
snuff film about death and bad owners,
the bodies everywhere, a dog
and cat massacre. Our kids' eyes
distend like goldfish—all that blood—
but they don't get it, how the life
escapes, how the work is to keep
it in, a finger for each vent,
a face to show the questioner
who stands now tall in front of us,
who wants to know, *Are you ready?*

Translation

For G.

Sunday night, I've been called in,
translator, my colleague—friend—
in his kitchen, police lines
from and to, the busy ants
clutch a towel, an old shoe,
assembly lines, jaw to jaw
whispers pass like clues. We have

a cop shadow, young Saito,
fresh from abroad. Pen and pad
out, he wants to crack the case,
finish up. Eager mirror,
his lips move with ours, soundless,
like a lunatic's in love.
My friend presses a thick palm

hard to each eye, rubs as if
to erase, his lungs bellows,
rush of air in, out a howl,
which I interrupt later,
the captain come to report:
suicide. Nothing I've done
harder than to say just that.

Divorce Poem

April noon, a valley in snow country,
window panes open *pop-pop*, the breeze

weighted, pine, old ice off the hill tops,
the water-blistered fields. We're to air

things out, *hanashiai*—word meeting,
only it's all amiss, the cold, my

posture, *seiza*—legs folded under,
ominously numb. Father-in-law

wants everything, so it's unanimous,
I'm to get the dog but nothing else.

Outside, the still-winter garden, the odd,
arthritic twists, the lifting up. *Jinsei*

ha kore kara—life is from now,
he tells me, the skin on his face and hands

taut, his kidneys are broken, daily
he grows larger, younger, a balloon

animal. If I could, I would rise up
and hit anything, my feet distant,

bloodless—how relentless the needs
of the body, how it fails us.

The Almost Deer

In the late 1980s, statues of wild animals were placed on riverbanks in the Kyoto area to provide a more natural feel.

Water to the knees, but no stoop
to this stone-snouted doe, bat ears
cupped up, flesh paint still from the high
water mark, but underneath bared
to the cement core. *Shizenka*,
our prefecture's natural-
ization project, which means dams,
great rock banks plumed with imported
grass, swing and slide sets, a jungle
gym. In a yet neglected copse
almost deer cools her hooves, willow
and bamboo about, the summer
light divides into fireflies,
into sub-hues and long shimmers,
everything on inhale, wind-brushed,
released from time. And the soul then,
what a thicket it must live in.

Cleaning Up

I fill boxes
until I'm out of boxes
and I lie on the floor
waiting for my brother to come,
waiting for more boxes.

My wife was thorough. There's nothing
of theirs, not a toy, not a sock,
not a hair. Later, I may admire her
efficiency, how after ten years,
she could move so easily,
removing excess with a surgeon's skill,
until I am left,
must pack my stuff, must leave
our home by tomorrow.

Now,
lying on the bathroom floor,
I can think only
Where is my brother?, that I need more
boxes, as if enough can be found
to hold everything. This impossible
quiet, this emptiness
spreading through our house
and I can think only,
I need more boxes.

On My Interview with the Sumo Wrestler at the Coin Laundromat Near My Apartment

He was impossibly big,
wider than the two tiny washers
that chugged and glugged
so precariously on all my clothes,
and which became his seat,
one for each cheek. My place
was on the windowsill—
there was nowhere else—
and I watched him like a crow would,
suspicious, ready to fly
if he became violent, curious
as to what might fall
from his lips.
He said two things to me.
The first was to ask for tobacco,
but I do not smoke. Then,
after ten minutes of silent
courage-summoning, I asked him
in my most formal Japanese
what it was like, meaning
the whole shebang, fame
and freakishness, sex object,
and spectacle. *Fuck off,*
faggot, he told me, the words
filling the room
like a fart.

Late

Mother on the phone again, not
yet sure where I'm at, the map out,
Fox News on. Thinks I should return,
that the waters have turned restless,
that it's another Chernobyl
and I'm already dead, poisoned
inside and out, a Japanese-
talking corpse. God has spoken, says
I backed the wrong country, the wrong
woman, the better values won—
how we justify disaster,
that it's earned, that it's not coming
for us next. I would tell her this,
but then she says it much better,
Sometimes, you understand too late
and there's nothing worse than too late.

Home Visit

Oya—parent, *needle*
with sharp eyes, but I see
no good end, plane going

nowhere, typhoon a hum,
shudder, a grey curtain
strung across the tarmac.

My son and I, our first
trip ever, America-
bound maybe, wanting what,

a miracle? *Need tea?*
asks the stewardess, still
fresh somehow in this our

second hour. His mother
called suddenly, said he'd
stopped school, talking, eating—

bullies but what to do?
I look at him, ten months
since we've last met, and how

smoothly I'm fifteen, zits
neon on my face, chest
sunken like a soup bowl,

knees knobby and awkward
as California oak.
But he's not me, and I

now don't know what to say,
strangers, his silence a
mouth, taking my words in,

reducing them. Outside,
two trucks cut a straight path
through the water, white lines

parallel, gone. In my
dreams I storm into school,
huge, foreign avenger,

or better that one friend
we all need. Cleared to go,
I talk on and on, the

trip, weather, scared of the
quiet, how when lost some
call out, some stay silent

and are never found.

North Mountain

A right turn, then another
and suddenly you're rising
out of this city, a road
paved yet no cars, green-quilted
canopy of sugi, elm,
a whisper in deep shadow,
stream unseen to the left. I
am running, the road corkscrews
above Takamatsu Lake,
the first clearing a farm house
abandoned, two bouquets left
each Saturday morning at
the family grave, lilies,
pale chrysanthemums, orchids—
always white, color of salt,
of death. Further, the forest
peels back, a single stone stood
on its narrow tip, *shihi*—
poem carved in the face—*Grace
of clouds in pale sky*, it says.
*I called for light here,
over my valley. It came.*

Dusk now, sky
the mirror's silver,
which forgets.

3

夢で言葉を飾るなら、まづ、愛と沈黙とびおろんの弦のごとく貫く光。

If you must decorate the word with dream, first write of love
and silence and light as piercing as a single string of the violin.

—Yamamura Bochou

Character Readings

The key to successful study of kanji lies in breaking down the barrier of unfamiliarity. Once one can appreciate how a character is made up, how it acquired its shape and why it came into existence, then one is a long way towards achieving this end.

—Kenneth Henshall

Here

     speak

        is a needle

            balanced   pin up

        on the tongue

    word

        the miracle

           a leaf

              that unfurls later

        in the heart

Here

     the two readings of *truth*

        a ripe field ready to cut

        a person hung by the feet

                        dead

     for not saying

              is the flower

       that opens

           in the next day's

    quiet

Here
    face
        is a canvas others write on
          thin
            the ideal skin
         wide
           for art must be seen
                palimpsest
     above a dream of body
the work waits

Virtual Idol

On June 20, 2011, Glico confirmed that Eguchi Aimi, the extremely popular new member of the pop band AKB48, was in fact a computer-generated creation, her face and body a composite taken from other band members.

From the start a paste
job, Mayu's eyebrows
arched like a cat's back,
Yuko's unwieldy
tits, the fleshy V
they made as she leaned
and leaned in her mom's
blue blouse, Mari's mouth,
scar just above the
kisser. The breakdown
is on the website,
scientific how
they fooled us, even
her voice a cocktail
nobody admits
to liking now. Her
posters taken down
fold into tiny
squares as if never
there.

Fish

            Left
always left
        until she comes
            full circle
                            her pupils wide from the painkillers,
like a fish's
        staring everywhere.

Brain tumor
says my host
            we drink Asahi Draft
                        watch the decaying
        orbit of the dog.

My host is a fish
            scientist
                        which is like a poet
    in water
        except afterward
        he eats
        his subjects raw.

Round and round the dog goes
        sight now a single pea
        only she can see
                The doctor wants to put her down
                says my host
                        but what kind of animal
                        would do that?

I am dating
　　　the daughter
　　　　　　　she sits to the side
　　　　　　　　　face tipped down
　　　the web of her left
　　　hand
　　　　　　just covers
　　　　　　her eyes.

They want to know my prospects
　　　at home I eat shoku-pan
　　　　　　　just ten yen a slice
　　　white Thai rice
　　　fat Japanese
　　　　　　radish
　　　tofu browned
　　　　　in miso sauce
　　　　　　　　cheap
　　　　　　　　　because all
　　　the author's copies in the world
　　　can't buy a single fish.

He has prepared a special
　　　treat
　　　　　from Taiji
　　　　　　　　raw whale
　　Sakana no isshu da yo
　　It's just another fish
　　　　　he says again
　　　　　and again
　　　　　　　Eat! Eat!

41

The Mom *tsks tsks*
    at my words
             like the flick
      of a scaled
    tail in water
        You've a beautiful house
           tsk tsk
        It's cold outside
           tsk tsk
        Time to go
           tsk tsk
    I want to say
             three hundred miles away
                   in another country
        they eat dog
        speared on short sticks.

The flesh is fatty pink
             smell of mowed grass
    taste of olive oil
        they all watch
                   their mouths move
                   with my mouth
        chew
            chew
      echo
          echo.

Outside
    the wind blows
        snow into white lines
so straight
    you wonder
        if they will fall at all.

Later
      when they are not looking
           I cup the rest
                lean down
                time it just
right
           the dog's mouth
                opens like a shark's
grateful
yet sly
           that last glance up.

Founders' Day Parade in Aurora, Utah

It would not do to say
the rain finished it,
though it seemed as plain

as the dull water-
shedding clouds that we
could go no further.

Oh Lord, we try to hold
the proper course, but when
will come the time to mend

our brokenness, the loss
of that which to us
is sacred? Will our last

breath be nothing but this?
I watched the crowd unfurl
like a lie discovered,

with not a story told
to mark its passing,
the long procession

a final shrivening,
a silent amen from
the dying to the dead.

Until the wide street
was cleansed of those
who would walk it,

and the empty road
fed the sky with grey,
the one streetlight red,
blinking in dismay.

Christmas Eve, 1973

Ah the untying, a loop of ribbon slipped,
the cackle of wrappings as we worked,
freeing corners from their snares. In the soft
twilight of two dull lamps we counted coup,
sleep seemed like death or worse, and as unlikely.
And we believed everything, the sigh a sleigh
makes in the air, gifts sprung sudden as mushrooms,
how we'd been just enough—what? *Bad* or *good*,
words we were dressed up in, like *divorce*,
names for things still lacking taste or touch.
Later, sent to bed but bigger than that,
hating it, I braved the dark and stole back
to a silver rain suspended, branches
weighted, like thumbs pointed down. You lay at
the foot. I remember all that you said,
sad supplicant, prone, wishing to be dead.

Arizona Rain

All simper and toupee, our guide
understands, takes us
down the gold hallway, the rubber fruit,
the Elvis-Jesus, acrylic
curly locks, halo cunningly
cocked, hands on the air guitar.
Low stage and a long box,
the face rouged-up, eye shadow,
warm latte lipstick—I recognize nothing,
he looks beautiful.

Twenty years, then thirty hours
home, a hospital room
shared, one white curtain, no bowel
control, voice, consciousness, *Your call*
80 breaths a minute and still
no air
how unfair.

I'm to say a few words,
thin structures of sound,
word a poor house,
a wicked pack,
the hand unplayable.
He was not
good,
though I will share here
one story to explain him.
His parents, wanting
to teach respect
character
would lock him and his brothers

in a basement cage,
lights out, a single dog bowl
filled with water. They couldn't
get out fast enough,
lying about their ages
to fight in Korea.

We are born too for this,
a key that turns in the door
once and only once. I
have stood outside
in my dreams, that darkness,
the body's weight
on the unseen ground,
how long the sound
of the closing lock
lingers in silence.

I wanted to know you better.
The next day, we drive
my father to the desert cemetery,
creosote scent of menthol
and cinnamon, barrel
cacti like squat stools, soil
hard, red-tinged—a long wait,
the honor guard late
as it rains and rains.

First Class

Chance neighbors, I on by voucher,
two flights cancelled, luggage in Guam,
pennies for breath, trout underarms,
and now a chair-bed, champagne glass,
theater attached to a remote
festooned, all buttons and arrows,
a game switch, a steward who says
to call him *Bob*. We're to Tokyo,
twelve hours to go and my neighbor,
who's seen it all, tells me about
it, the *they* who keep down the *we*,
black presidents, taxes and tea,
women with no interest in sex,
me, even the Constitution.
When I close my eyes, two sleepless
nights stream in playback, a private
home for the blind where things are cursed.
The man fancies us a kind, class
mates, takes out slippers, a lemon
cookie, adjusts each breast-dumpling.
Their loss, he says, meaning the country,
wants a response, but unsteady
I, one eye on the dinner trays
advancing like hope, say nothing;
which makes me different, or worse.

Ex

Damn that long-fingered hand,
the lucky apricots
squeezed, squeezed, a juicy test,
that one ungiving, this
gone too slack, how texture
becomes taste, that final
feel in the mouth when all's
ripe. Our eyes meet again,
ten years later, only
pineapples between us.
The mind jumps, nervous thing—
thorny fruit, the sour
tongue curled, clumsy, *hello*,
no, go—all I should have
said a wasp inside, sharp
needle primed, plump to burst.

Landscape with Cherry Blossoms

We hurry out, dog with a low whine, a look back,
somewhere a disconnect, new snow now, the white flags
of our breaths, and yet this narrow lane framed,
hooded by thousands of pale flowers, salmon-cheeked,
the soft insides of conch shells, that certain May air,
savory, like how a perfume applied just right
makes up for everything. First up, ours the sole
sounds, echo to each step, dog warming to the task,
trailblazers, moonlight behind when suddenly
a tea rose rises on the horizon. It's then
we see her, beyond the hedges thin as penwork,
the round-ridged houses, the terrible perfection
of morning, at the tree marking our turn home,
a single statue, snow-laced, the young girl long dead,
hands joined, a prayer, a stone cup filling with spring.

Kathmandu in the Time of Cholera

> This is the truth:
> There is nothing to accept,
> nothing to reject.
> —Ashtavakra Gita 6:1

I

Already ill, done
in by raw carrots
and milk tea, I see
a beggar girl lean
inside the cab, one
eye, a long finger
pointing, face angled
to show the scar, her
money spot. *Please*, she
says, as the car moves.

II

Into light and back,
thoughts on a thin thread,
cat-curled, a soft seat.
What is it in the
air or the water
caught on the branches
of the brown winter
roses? Sour-sweet,
sky's gasoline scent,
shadows of mountains.

III

The driver transforms
in my fever, crazed,
heroic. No speed
limits, painted lanes,
no street lights (power
out two years), he stops
once, five boys, three dogs
larger still, looking
for home. *I've seen worse*,
he says suddenly.

IV

From *The Kathmandu Post* (March 21, 2009):

*It is a sobering fact for a country rich in water resources that nearly
10,500 children lose their lives each year owing to lack of clean drinking
water and proper sanitation.*

V

I'm to give a speech—
literacy—but
the letters gyrate,
saucy lines, the shapes
astonishing. What
links us, here before
the door that opens
on my story? Freed;
generator down,
the room lights blink out.

VI

One last memory,
a night wait, car late
to the hospital,
I see the boys, dogs
together for warmth,
heads in a circle,
leg petals, a street
flower, tough, the kind
that sprouts in the cracks,
whose sole name is *love*.

Biwa Blues

Aoi, adj. 1. *Life in a well or bowl.*
　　　　　 2. *The color blue.*
　　　　　 3. *The color green (as in* start *or* go).

Straight shot, a bullet
train through three hours
of tunnels then sun
like a strobe light, there
a stream under us
white-tailed, breathless leap
from rock to rock, here
a village locked out,
four houses, valley
snow-capped and endless.
Startled, a man waves,
grandfather, blur, then
clear, six months after
everything, even
the season different,
rice top-heavy, field
after field of bowed
heads bronzed for harvest.
Outside, my station,
new home, everything
in one knapsack I
taste the miracle,
a rain untainted,
think of the tribe whose
dances never fail
for they keep dancing
till they sight the deer,
how so much depends

on finding the right
bus. May all of us
arrive finally
where we are needed—
ahead a huge lake,
Biwa-ko, God's Lute,
sky and water one
color, meeting point
unseen, infinite,
blue.

Campfire

For E.

Slow into night goes
the leaving, the dull rise
of smoke reaching upward
from our last wood.
Already, the circle deepens
about us, this shell of day
we cling to, our small fire
stubborn yet against the long
liquid pull of evening.
Then, through our thin tent,
the cold's soft whisper...
It's done. It's done.

Notes

The book's title comes from the official government designation for this region—豪雪地帯 or "the region of deep snows." The first epigraph is taken from a poem by Ibaraki Noriko titled わたしが一番きれいだったとき. It relates her experiences as a teenager during and right after WW2.

Miyako, Yamada, and Otsuchi are the names of cities in Iwate Prefecture, Japan. They were heavily damaged during the 2011 earthquake/tsunami.

In "Maho no Kotoba," the initial italicized word is the Japanese greeting or honorific phrase, with the italicized word(s) that follow the translation.

Regarding "Fly-jin," "jin" means "person" in Japanese, while "fly" is a play on (and rhymes with) "gai," or "foreign. "

Note that "nisshoku," the Japanese word for "eclipse," literally does mean "the sun eating."

As suggested in "The Memory of Now," alternate light sources, including strobe lights powered by portable generators and even candles, were used to provide night illumination on local roads until power could be rerouted to the disaster zone.

In the poem "Afterward," the character 再 (pronounced "sigh") means "again."

Some of the key terms in "For They Are Coming," "Booze Well," and "Character Readings" are represented in Japanese by characters that originally were ideographs depicting incidents/relationships loosely along the lines described. E.g., the characters making up the word "communication" (伝達) really did originally refer to "lightning" and "a field," and the characters for "truth" (真実) really did originally depict "a prisoner hung up by the heels dead" and "a field ready for harvest" respectively. Of course, as in these examples, the characters have become so stylized over time (two thousand years) that their former meanings are not readily recognizable today.

The term "shihi" (詩碑) in "North Mountain" refers to a monument to an author, usually a single stone inscribed with a poem or (rarely) a short prose quotation. The *shihi* described in my poem is dedicated to, and contains a poem by, Tachihara Michizo—a Japanese poet who died of tuberculosis in 1939 (at the age of 24).

Japan uses "research" as a cover for its ongoing whaling industry, with the participating scientists being paid in free whale/porpoise meat as well...as I learned during the events depicted in "Fish."

As noted in "Biwa Blues," "aoi" means both "blue" and "green" in Japanese. The first definition refers to the original meaning of the ideograph itself. The italicized quotation is taken from Heaney's *Station Island*.

Acknowledgments

Grateful acknowledgment is made to the editors of the following publications in which these poems first appeared:

Agni: "For They Are Coming," "The Author, Taken by His Boss to the Baths, Receives an Instructional Brochure," "Knuckleheads," "Ex"

Beloit Poetry Journal: "Character Readings"

The Cape Rock: "Gomi Station," "Virtual Idol"

Cimarron Review: "Dog"

FIELD: "North Mountain," "Divorce Poem," "Eclipse," "The Memory of Now"

Michigan Quarterly Review: "How Not to Find a Body," "Quake"

The Missouri Review: "Fall"

Poetry East: "Almost Deer," "Fly-jin," "Afterward," "Tanka at the End of Everything"

REAL: "Founders' Day Parade in Aurora, Utah," "Fish"

Snake Nation Review: "Landscape with Cherry Blossoms," "Maho no Kotoba"

Spillway: "Kathmandu in the Time of Cholera," "Biwa Blues"

A number of these poems also appeared in *Character Readings*, a collection which won the 2011 Copperdome Poetry Chapbook Prize.

The FIELD Poetry Series